Bible sleuth

New Testament

ILLUSTRATED BY
JOSÉ PÉREZ MONTERO

TYNDALE
K!DS

Tyndale House Publishers, Inc.
Carol Stream, IL

Hi there! I'm Mike. I love adventures and going back in time. I'm especially fond of going back in biblical times and witnessing some of the most exciting events in history. Are you good at finding things? If you are, I'd love to bring you along on another adventure. We'll do some investigating, and you'll be an expert Bible Sleuth by the end of our journey.

Here are a few things you should know before we go: as you read the stories, try to find the pictures in the sidebar in each scene. When you find each clue, you'll learn a little more about the colorful, dramatic, and sometimes chaotic biblical world. You'll see funny or surprising things along the way—some will make you laugh; others might make your jaw drop. It's all part of the fun as we go through the New Testament together.

The Birth of Jesus

When Mary was expecting Baby Jesus, Joseph and Mary traveled to Bethlehem to register in the census. There was no place to stay for the night, so they slept in a stable. That night, Jesus was born. Some shepherds, who were watching their sheep nearby, saw a choir of angels singing, and the angels told them the Savior of the world had been born. The shepherds hurried away and found Mary, Joseph, and Baby Jesus in the stable, and they worshiped God.

See Luke 2:1-20.

Jesus at the Temple

When Jesus was twelve, His family celebrated Passover in Jerusalem. Afterward, the family set off on a long journey to go back home again. Jesus, however, stayed behind in the Temple, but Mary and Joseph didn't notice. After a day, Mary and Joseph started looking for Jesus and found Him three days later at the Temple all the way back in Jerusalem. There He was, speaking to the religious leaders. "Jesus," His mother said. "We were worried sick!" Jesus answered, "Didn't you know I would be in my Father's house?" *See Luke 2:41-49.*

The Wedding at Cana

As an adult, Jesus attended a wedding in a town called Cana. During the festivities, the wine suddenly ran out, and Jesus' mother, Mary, said to her son, "They've run out of wine." Jesus directed servants to fill large jugs with water. When they had poured some, they brought it to the host. The host tasted the water, then said to the bridegroom, "This wine is much better than the one we had before!" The water from the large jugs had been turned into delicious wine. When Jesus' disciples saw this, they believed that He was the Son of God. *See John 2:1-11.*

Jesus Clears the Temple

It was almost time to celebrate Passover, so Jesus traveled to Jerusalem. When He went to the Temple, He became angry. The Temple courts were full of merchants selling sheep and cattle for the offerings, and other men had set up tables to exchange money. Jesus made a whip and chased them out of the Temple. He turned the money tables over, sending coins clattering to the floor. "Get this stuff out of here!" Jesus yelled. "You have turned My Father's house into a marketplace, when it is supposed to be a house of prayer!"

See Matthew 21:12-13 ; John 2:13-16.

Look for:

Jesus Heals a Paralyzed Man

Four men carried their paralyzed friend on a mat to Jesus so He could heal him, but they couldn't get through the crowd in the house where Jesus was teaching. So they made a hole in the roof and lowered their friend down to Jesus. Jesus saw their faith and said to the paralyzed man, "Your sins are forgiven. Get up and walk." And to everyone's amazement, the paralyzed man stood up, took his mat, and went home praising God.

See Mark 2:1-12.

The Beatitudes

Jesus sat on a hill, teaching. He said, "Happy are those who realize their need for God. They will live in God's Kingdom. Happy are those who are sad. God will comfort them. Happy are those who do right. God will give them a satisfied heart. Some people will say bad things about you because you belong to Me, but be happy because you will be rewarded in Heaven when you hold on to Me no matter what."

See Matthew 5:1-12.

A Sick Woman

Jesus was in the middle of a large crowd. A woman in the crowd had been sick for twelve years and no doctor could help her. She thought if she could only touch Jesus' coat, she would be healed. She touched it and felt her body heal instantly. "Who touched me?" Jesus asked. The woman was afraid, but she knelt before Him trembling and told Him her story. Jesus said, "Dear woman, you're healed because you believed." See Mark 5:24-34.

Look for:

Jesus Feeds the Five Thousand

When Jesus finished teaching the crowd of people, it was dinnertime. The disciples wanted to send the people home to get food, but Jesus had another plan. With only five loaves of bread and two fish, Jesus and the disciples miraculously fed more than five thousand people.   *See Mark 6:30-44.*

Zacchaeus the Tax Collector

Zacchaeus climbed a tree to see Jesus. As Jesus passed through, He looked up and said, "Zacchaeus, come down. I'm coming to your house today." Zacchaeus was thrilled, but people complained that Jesus was staying with a sinner. Zacchaeus said, "I will give half of everything I have to the poor, and if I cheated anyone, I'll give him back four times what I stole." See Luke 19:1-10.

The Triumphal Entry

The crowd heard Jesus was coming to Jerusalem, riding on a colt. They grabbed palm branches and ran to meet Him. The people waved their branches and shouted, "God bless the One who comes in the name of the Lord!" But the Pharisees were upset because the people were following Jesus instead of them.

See John 12:12-19.

Look for:

21

The Holy Spirit Comes at Pentecost

After Jesus rose from the dead and returned to heaven, the apostles gathered together on the Day of Pentecost. Suddenly, they heard a strong wind, and flames settled over each of them. The Holy Spirit had come. He gave them the power to speak other languages. People were amazed that they could understand in their own language what the disciples taught about God. See Acts 2:1-11.

Look for:

The Apostles Heal Many

The apostles of Jesus were performing many miracles. They gathered at the Temple, and people brought them the sick. Peter and the apostles healed them through Jesus' power. Because of these miracles, more and more people believed in Jesus and became part of the group of believers, who would later be called Christians.   See Acts 5:12-16.

Stephen

God helped Stephen perform many miracles, but some men didn't like him. Because they couldn't find anything to accuse him of, these men paid people to lie about Stephen, and so he was killed for something he didn't do. Even while people were throwing stones at Stephen to kill him, he asked God to forgive them.   *See Acts 6:8-15; 7:54-60.*

A Crowd of People Praising God

God gave John a vision of heaven. A large crowd of people praised God, saying, "Hallelujah! Our God rules. Let us be happy and give God glory." An angel told John to write, "Those who are invited to be with Jesus are blessed." The angel said, "These are the true words of God."

See Revelation 19:6-9.

Visit Tyndale's website for kids at www.tyndale.com/kids.

TYNDALE is a registered trademark of Tyndale House Publishers, Inc. The Tyndale Kids logo is a trademark of Tyndale House Publishers, Inc.

Bible Sleuth: New Testament

Original edition published in Denmark under the title *Bible Detective* by Scandinavia Publishing House, Copenhagen, Denmark.

Copyright © 2017 by Scandinavia Publishing House. All rights reserved.

Previously published as *Bible Detective: Looking for Jesus* (ISBN 9788771328356) and *Bible Detective: Looking for the First Christians* (ISBN 9788771328363) by Scandinavia Publishing House. First printing by Tyndale House Publishers, Inc., in 2017.

Text by Vanessa Carroll

Designed by Gao Hanyu, Li Dan

Illustrated by José Pérez Montero.
Cover illustration of index cards copyright © Harper 3D/Shutterstock. All rights reserved.
Cover illustration of paperclip note copyright © Yurlick/Shutterstock. All rights reserved.

Edited by Cecilie Fodor

For manufacturing information regarding this product, please call 1-800-323-9400.

ISBN 978-1-4964-2243-9
Printed in China

23   22   21   20   19   18   17
7   6   5   4   3   2   1